COMMENTS BY READERS

"This book is not only fun to read...it is an inspiration...I love this book and highly recommend it." Mary P.

"I am savoring your book...reading a chapter at a time and loving it." Donna P.

"Thank you for bringing heaven down to earth!" Paul M.

"Glenn takes the wonderful life lessons and inspiration we receive from dancing and expresses them in a thought provoking way. I highly recommend this book...!" Carrie K.

"I adore your book, your style, sensitivity..." Darlene D.

"Thank you for writing your book! Your thoughts and words will bring joy to many dancers." Shirley M.

"If you are satisfied with candy bars then this book may not be for you. But if your taste runs to gourmet, melt-in-your-heart morsels of delight, then this beautifully written book is for you." Rosemary W.

"Thoughtful, expressive, even humorous at times. Opened me to a new attitude about dance, and life." Linda P.

"Beautifully written! This book describes ballroom dance in a way I've always felt, but couldn't put into words..." Karen S.

Three Minutes to Heaven

Musings of a Ballroom Dancer

GLENN A. WALKER

Three Minutes to Heaven
Musings of a Ballroom Dancer
(2nd edition)

Copyright © 2023 by Glenn A. Walker
All Rights Reserved

No part of this book may be reproduced, stored in a retrieval system, or transmitted by any means without the written permission of the author and publisher.

Collins-Wellesley Publishing
Author contact: glennw@san.rr.com
https://www.facebook.com/ThreeMinutesToHeaven

ISBN: 978-0-9652591-6-3

Library of Congress Control Number: 2023905464

PUBLISHED IN THE
UNITED STATES OF AMERICA

"God is a DJ ... Life is a dance floor"
   --Pink, 2009

Table of Contents

Chapter 1: Changing Times 5

Chapter 2: Going With the Flow 9

Chapter 3: Hi, My Name is Dance. Welcome
            to My Home. 13

Chapter 4: Cornfields and Foxtrots. 17

Chapter 5: Nature's Song. 21

Chapter 6: Angels on the Horizon. 25

Chapter 7: The Quiet Voice Inside. 28

Chapter 8: Foundations. 31

Chapter 9: Syncing with the Universe. 36

Chapter 10: The Nature of Beauty. 40

Chapter 11: Hey, By the Way, Thanks!. 45

Chapter 12: Rubbing Your Feet. 48

Chapter 13: The Tao of Dance. 53

Chapter 14: Soap Bubbles and Phantoms. 56

Chapter 15: Imagine. 60

Chapter 16: On Dance (the missing chapter from
Kahlil Gibran's "The Prophet")............62

Chapter 17: 'Selfish' Giving......................65

Chapter 18: The Beauty of Entanglement..........68

Chapter 19: Monster in the Mirror................74

Chapter 20: Guru of Dance.......................77

Chapter 21: Words Can't Describe................81

Chapter 22: Showcase at the Seashore............85

Chapter 23: The Spirit of Dance..................88

Chapter 24: The Dancing Trees....................93

Chapter 25: Long Ago and Far Away..............96

Chapter 26: Finding Your Elegant Moments........99

Chapter 27: The Need to Give...................103

Chapter 28: That Certain Kind of Dance..........106

Chapter 29: One Step at a Time.................109

Chapter 30: Dancing with the Whole Brain........112

Chapter 31: Dancer as Actor....................115

Chapter 32: The Valley of Perpetual Dance.......118

Chapter 33: Having a 'Plan B'...................121

Chapter 34: You Are What You Dance! 124

Chapter 35: The Gift of a Challenge. 127

Chapter 36: Not What it May Seem. 130

Chapter 37: Making it Your Own. 134

Chapter 38: The Timeless Dance. 138

Chapter 39: From Deprivation Arises Gratitude. 141

Chapter 40: The Night the Dancing Died. 145

Foreword

On the surface, flying a kite, getting a foot massage, and blowing soap bubbles seem to have little to do with ballroom dancing. And knot theory and string theory are the farthest thing from a dancer's mind. But there are often threads that connect widely disparate activities in which we routinely engage, even as the universe presents us with many clues of the presence of a ubiquitous but little-understood unifying element guiding all of the natural processes of existence. This book draws attention to some of these connections, and to the analogous qualities of dance and everyday life. Sometimes it's the little things that shine a light on their more important counterparts.

The following is a portion of the introduction I offer in the first edition: *"Life is but a spiritual dance.*

Learning to live well has much in common with learning to dance well. And we learn to dance by starting with a curiosity and an open mind, much like children trying to discover what life is about. As you grow in dance, you learn an appreciation and love of it as it becomes a greater part of your life, just as you learn to love life as you grow and sample the rich palette of experiences life has to offer.

"The love of dance germinates many offshoots, one of which is helping you build a place deep within your being a sacred and personal place of retreat that offers comfort and tremendous joy. It is a place of safety and healing, and in time, a place to which you want to invite that special dance partner. Once that infrastructure is established, it often takes only three minutes to get there – the length of a typical ballroom dance song.

"Dance can bring such a joy, and in the process, helps color your vision of how you want to live your life. It helps you reflect on life lessons, things you've experienced and others you've missed. Dance, like life, is all about attitude and flow. Grace, whether in dance or in life, happens when you approach every situation with an open mind and are present in the moment. The attitude of accepting what is without a struggle

results in a harmonious flow which, in turn, reinforces the attitude. When conflict appears, it's often a matter of a simple attitude adjustment to reestablish the grace and flow.

"Because of the many opportunities we are offered to extend the things we learn in dance to everyday life, in a way dance can be looked at as a microcosm of life in general. Dance has the capacity to tear you apart, then rebuild you from the ground up. It is a constant process of self-discovery and adjustment with lessons in patience, humility, appreciation, perseverance, awareness, and pride of accomplishment."

The act of being mindful in everyday living requires the same awareness we appeal to in order to dance with the beat and phrasing of the music. The chapters of this book represent a collection, in no particular order, of my writings during my dance experience, now into its 3rd decade. This updated edition includes several new chapters, and my hope is that at least one will touch you in some special way, whether it's on the ballroom floor... or on the path of life's journey!

Glenn Walker, 2023

Chapter 1

Changing Times

Times change. I remember the old days when drivers would stop for pedestrians and cashiers would offer a smile to their customers. Times when a man's word was as solid as stone, and a handshake as good as a signed contract. They were simpler times when the humble, the modest, the thoughtful outnumbered the haughty, the brazen, the rash. They were times when the winners were esteemed and rewarded on merit, and those who came in second were encouraged to try harder. They were nobler times when men aspired to be gentlemen, and ladies did not so quickly shove aside their femininity. Conceivably, someone could have been writing this a generation ago about their own youth as well. Times continue their change.

Today, we are met with the challenges living in societies with rapidly growing populations. As more of us seek scarcer resources, we sometimes step on each other to be first in line. We live in a modern world of drugs and chemicals and disposables. We become conditioned to not care anymore. If our bodies ail, there's a drug we can take. If something doesn't appeal to our natural senses, we alter it with chemicals. If something breaks, we toss it out and buy a new one. Why care for what we have when things are so dispensable? Yet our spiritual culture has become so infested with much the same attitude that we often discard the very things that are integral to our quintessential beings, sometimes with a numbed awareness.

When I was in school, there were no classes on the etiquette of human living, or how to be a gentleman. If you look at schools today, can one really expect students to learn to be courteous, kind, and respectful when teachers must spend their time trying to keep guns from the classroom and drugs from the lockers? Times have changed. But today, as always, the best teaching is the example we each set, and yes, we are all teachers. Opportunities abound for us to play a starring role as a mentor, just by our own actions.

Isn't it great that ballroom dance can – even for a few moments – take us away from the world we have become, and let us again be ladies and gentlemen? Dance instructors don't often teach etiquette or gentlemanly manners, except by their own behavior, which students – like curious children – so readily want to emulate.

I remember having the privilege of sitting at the same table as my instructor when attending one of my first formal ballroom parties. His tuxedo was perfect, and he always stood when a lady approached the table, greeting her or holding her chair. I had another instructor who developed terminal cancer, yet he continued showing up for his lessons on time and teaching with energy and verve with no complaints despite the physical tolls of chemotherapy treatment. Sometimes, not a word need be said to teach. Actions do speak, sometimes louder than we know, and we do learn well by example from those we look up to.

As ballroom dancers, we are constantly surrounded by nice people. We could so easily take the conduct we learn in dance out to our everyday lives, and make the world a little better with our kind actions. Such opportunities confront us daily, so why not grab them, and be ladies and gentlemen in the dance of life?

Yes, times do change. But we would hope for the better. A simple act of random kindness may not always appear to make much difference. But it can be quite infectious – and maybe even start a process that could end up changing the world...

CHAPTER

2

Going With the Flow

When you show up for the first time at the dance studio eager to learn how to dance, you have no idea how your life is about to change! But that's a good thing. You're entering a territory with twists and turns and no clue whether joy or terror awaits you around the next curve. But you take one step at a time. Learning to dance is a process with many phases, and each phase has many steps. The first step is learning to walk through a basic dance pattern to the beat of the music. And as you do, you feel more confident that terror is not what's likely lurking ahead!

So you begin. You might look at the initial phase as learning some of the elementary movements of dance. You learn about posture and body positions. You learn about your frame and how it relates to your partner. You absorb as much as you can, and practice often. As you add more patterns, you start to pay attention to the technique: when to step on your heel or the ball of your foot, when to open or close your frame, when to step between your partner's feet and when to step outside partner. And you'll continue to experiment with your partner connection until it "feels right". As you go to more dance socials, you'll want to learn floorcraft, which includes having a number of different options following any dance pattern you do to facilitate safely navigating around a crowded floor. Along the way, you'll pick up some of the history and tradition of ballroom dancing and learn about dance etiquette.

The next phases might include learning head turns and arm styling and dance lines and shadow positions and syncopations. When your dancing develops a greater level of sophistication, you'll want to focus on musicality and temperament, how your dancing mirrors your interpretation of the music, when to add power for dynamic moves and when to slow down for moments of grace. You'll want to study the music, and pay attention to the phrasing. Ultimately, you'll put all of these things together, and then you'll be called 'a dancer'.

Each phase of learning is a segment you go through that builds a foundation for the next phase. And that transition from phase to phase is marked by pride in accomplishment and gratitude of the growth you experience. You don't look back with sorrow at what you've forgotten or lost, rather you look forward to the gifts of learning – or relearning – those things that constantly shower your life. What is a cloud but a different form of the lake's water which evaporated to form it? Likewise, you become a different form of who you are, shaped by the absorption of dance. The ultimate realization is one of a seamless process that takes differing forms in an endless cycle.

As the cloud moves through the atmosphere, eventually raining down to wash the earth and provide moisture for its plants before finally running off to the streams and rivers which empty back into the lake. Each of those phases is a different form of something much bigger as the cycle unfolds. The process of dancing is much the same and has an order to the cycle. It can't rain until the cloud first forms. And it's hard to dance with grace until you've learned the partner connection. Each phase presents a different form of YOU as a dancer. But they're really all the same. YOU haven't changed, but simply have managed to express different forms of who you are.

Whatever phase of dancing you find yourself in, keep in mind it is a unique expression of a greater whole. Being mindful of the big picture that depicts a whole cycle as a series of phases will help you see the interdependency of the parts and how everything is connected in the cycle of life.

Chapter

3

Hi, My Name is "Dance". Welcome to My Home

You sought peace from the calamity, warmth from the storm, and ended up at my doorstep. You waited just on the other side of the threshold, but seemingly miles away. All you had to do was knock and it would open. You started by turning the page. And here you are!

Welcome. This is my home. A place where you can dream, and live the journey rather than the destination. Where you can replenish your desires, and take time to polish your dance shoes and study your class syllabus. Where the weight vanishes from your path's obstacles, and you are bathed in music-filled molecules floating everywhere in your midst. And that path is as bright as the sun each morning, and as strong as the blades of grass pushing up against a pounding rain.

My home offers you a safe place to build a nest for your soul. Here you can dream, and this dream becomes the life you live. My home is filled with furnishings like the morning sun, the sparrow in springtime finding its first worm, the smell of the garden after the evening's rain, the comfort of friendship, and a daily diet to build your confidence in executing a natural hover telemark while thinking about all that 'home' means.

Go ahead, look around. If you'd like a guided tour, the guides are these: the hardwood floor that supports your feet, the air that renews your every breath, and the music that keeps everything moving. In the living room you'll find the comfort of a burning fireplace in a winter storm. And in another room, a quiet sanctuary that the loudest of life's chaos cannot displace. Stepping through the hall, you'll chassé to the beat of syncopated chimes moving in a gentle ocean zephyr near a half open window. You'll find all the furnishings you need, and soon feel at home with a quick open reverse or syncopated hairpin. The dance you do, you learn here in my home. And it becomes the dream you live. It's just a matter of opening the door and again seeing for the first time.

When you pass the hallway mirror, you might see all those childhood worries buried in your eyes, and all the holding back that makes something in you die. Sometimes the memories come in bits and pieces, the longings you want to vividly recall. Some things you don't want to remember, and try so hard to cover with the rug in one room, in a drawer in another, under the duvet in still another. You mask the smell of your tears lying dormant, dried and yellowed on your pillow -- the very tears that tried to bring solace to your soul when those once thriving roots of a forever love, now lost, were wrenched from your heart. And sometimes when the memories hurt so much you no longer want to grow, then a guiding light leads you out from your dark hiding place and makes everything worthwhile. The innocence from your youth which had hardened again becomes pliable, your tenderness is resurrected from a deep sleep. You'll find lots of brightness here. Illuminating your steps even as you lilt to reach a dish from the cupboard, or do a turning lock to switch on the light.

My home will be like the tender hand gently embracing the trembling heart of a captive bird. You'll be safe in my presence, even with the storm outside – and the turbulence within that you've held so long. And once you've acclimated to all the comforts of home, you'll want nothing more than to give back the joy you've found with everything you touch.

It's so scary to open that door, but that's all it takes. Welcome to my home. It is where you may live. It is where you will eat and breathe and exist. The dreams inside are your sustenance, and the dance of life its essence. With it, all other desires will vanish.

Welcome. Now dance!

Chapter 4

Cornfields and Foxtrots

I remember the days of youth when we played in the cornfields and built tree forts in the woods. We'd lie around absorbing the days like there was a never-ending supply of them, not thinking much past lunchtime or beyond the corner store with its endless supply of penny candy sitting seductively behind the glass counter. You wonder how life can turn out so different than you once experienced, looking back at your days of wonder when lifetime dreams are formed and how those days morphed into a busy life with little time to reflect on them. You just never know the kind of dreams that will last, the ones you really want to hold onto, and those you can leave in the past with but a fond memory.

    Then you meet the life of dance, which many of us fall into like a child discovers a playground. We trade in romping in the cornfields and climbing trees to learning tipple chassés and impetus turns, and the candy behind the counter becomes the experience of tasting a simple social rumba or an engaging Dancesport competition. At some point we realize we're doing what we did as a child, just in a slightly different form.

    It seems like things are so different than they once were, wondering who we are now, and looking back to the person from whom we grew. Changing perceptions is just a part of living and growing – how you learn to follow your dreams and become who you are, yet still keep as sacred those parts that you let go – knowing that which you let go becomes the foundation of something new. And in the end, you finally connect them in a way that gives life a sense of coherence, flow, continuity, synergy.

Have you ever wondered how dance has changed you, the person you were before, and have become since? Scientists have shown that the human brain can be physically altered by the simple act of listening to music, and that the movement of dance results in an increase in endorphin levels raising one's pain threshold. Along with the physiologic changes from dancing, your life gently transforms, your outlook changes, your demeanor, your perceptions, confidence, mood, even your walk, your gait, your posture, your smile, your aura – all are subject to alteration from a steady diet of dance.

But a better question might be: have you ever wondered how dance has allowed you to rediscover the child in you who found that playground many years ago, and showed you the flow and continuity of a coherent life? Just as adulthood requires growing past childhood without forgetting it, the dance is a playful expression of a childhood activity found only in a formerly unrevealed dream. Life has so many stages, like the plant that flowers so beautifully, then drops its seeds into the soil fertilized by its own fallen leaves, and new life -- a new form emerges and builds on its foundation.

You breathe in the newness, and exhale that which bore the renewal, but the air is all the same – the playground is all that changed.

And this playground has music! Next time you dance a foxtrot, think about running as a child in the cornfields or weaving among the trees in the woods. For when we dance, it's a whisper of the old days we hold dear, simply calling us back to the playful child inside.

Chapter

5

Nature's Song

Y ou go through life and every now and then a magical moment comes along. That was the case for me last autumn, strolling under a clear sky with a tune I couldn't get out of my head. It was a day I followed nature's call of renewal, when I was to reclaim a sense of peace only the forest's beauty can provide. I found myself in a meadow of serenity punctuating a period of disquietude and self-doubt, a lake filled with still waters at rest after passing through the turbulent rapids.

Wandering through an ancient grove of giant Redwoods, I halted as a lone fawn, innocently stopped as if frozen in time, stared me in the eye. Then as if shrugging her shoulders, she meandered off toward a clearing by a stream. I watched for a time – it could have been minutes or hours – the solitary fawn going about her daily routine as if schedules, clocks and calendars didn't exist.

The setting was a perfect home for her, I thought -- but all alone. Where is her mother, her herd, her companions? Yet so content in aloneness, so at peace with her surroundings, such a fluid and graceful dance to the music of the birds, the breeze, the brook. Surrounded by a vibrant, living forest, she was far from alone, and I learned I wasn't either.

The moment vanished, the emptiness in my heart gradually filled with the experience of being among the abundance of nature. I lay down under the rising moon seeing my life much like I saw that fawn. What phantoms are woven into the music, inexorably drawing me from the herd, away from the crowd, far from the machinations of human life to one with no physical image? It's a different kind of song, one that requires a dance in the vast expanses away from the lives of noise, immersed in the peace of solitude, places where aloneness is a joy and time does not move. Life is a complex dance in a continuum uninterrupted by the fractured images of a changing kaleidoscope, no longer a black and white maze that keeps us going in circles.

But the dance goes with the music. The things which live in this forest speak to me like no human words ever could. The message is a song that makes me want to dance, the singer an unmistakable rhythm in the trees' silent infinity. It's a dance that brings joy uncluttered by noise, need, or pretenses, even as it devours itself in a curious world of wordless emotion. Some see it as a lonely life. But loneliness is nothing more than the elusive ability to connect the song of love with the dance of life.

And yes, there are times the darkness of night whacks me in the head asking if I'd trade a life of the mundane for a minute of this seeming abstraction, even as a chill bathes me in sorrow, infecting me with temporal desires. But invariably the music helps me find the dream again – that dream of the lovely fawn gracefully grazing, playfully dancing among the meadows and butterflies.

The sunlight caresses my eyelids awake, and I find myself again, in a resplendent stillness populated with entities that fit together like a finished puzzle, with a dance that goes with the song. The new music has come, and the choreography begins again. Noise turns to solitude, turbulence to peace.

The music is for finding the dream. The dance, for living it.

CHAPTER

6

Angels on the Horizon

The gray waters turn to dark blue and the white clouds turn to light blue, and then merge to a blending of the two most beautiful blues, as the clouds part, the mist dissipates and the water warms. Clarity is born of parting clouds, the sharp line that separates the ocean from the sky appears in its purest form. The horizon, that formless, figureless abstract phantom – that is where I see the angels dancing – so smoothly, freely gliding, almost like skating on the thin line which we seek but never attain.

One day as I peered out to the horizon on a clear day, there appeared silhouettes of the dancing angels doing what looked like a foxtrot, but maybe it was my imagination. I could have sworn I saw something that reminded me of a Fred Astaire movie in those silhouettes just before the sun was extinguished by the ocean. But you never know for sure from such a deceptive orb – one that at times creates eclipses, solar flares, and green flashes.

The Horizon is but a variegated phantom of fantasies – a place we hold dear to our imagination but can never touch. Nor can the sharks, nor the sea creatures, nor the dangers of the night. That nirvana is safe haven for the dancing angels. So why is it so far-fetched they would dance a foxtrot where the waters are most still?

Have you ever wondered what it would be like to dance so free from the perils that constantly threaten...the stormy waters that, for some reason, wish to quash the beauty of the movement before its denouement? Yet the sharks abound, and we constantly fend off their attacks just to get to that place where we can find our own sort of nirvana, a peaceful horizon within our emotions, a complacency within our dreams, a simple light of beauty to brighten the world. That is all most want: to experience a moment of freedom to dance on the horizon, and in the process to show the world just one ray of light before the sun sets.

That's why we dance. That's why we breathe...

CHAPTER

7

The Quiet Voice Inside

Have you ever heard a little voice inside you with a warning, a bit of advice, or just some expression of hesitation which you ignored, then later found yourself in trouble?

Your inner voice can be soft. To hear it well, you must quiet your mind. The voice inside is only as loud as your willingness to listen.

Your awareness of yourself, of others, of your surroundings, and of life in general is a key element of your spiritual nature, which in turn is only as strong as that voice is right.

When you ignore that little voice deep inside, but know that it has been right so often, you must start to trust in your own spiritual prescience. Some may call it intuition or insight or metaphysical intelligence, but these are just words for an enlightened state or a connectedness to all that is – 'mindfulness'.

If you've been dancing for a while, you've probably come to recognize dance as a microcosm of life. Those qualities that make us good dancers are the same qualities that help us grow as human beings. The awareness that helps us navigate around the dance floor avoiding collisions and projecting elegance is the same awareness that helps us become successful in all that we do. There's a way of perceiving and knowing that cannot be learned in school or by reading a book or going to a class. A sense of enlightenment is yours simply by quieting the mind, opening the soul, and allowing your inner voice to guide you.

The human brain is a master at quickly gathering information and, for the most part, subconsciously processing it in a way that guides our behavior. Despite good intentions, we would sometimes make a different decision if we had more information. That's where a keen sense of awareness comes in, enabling minute details to paint a more vivid picture of the information the brain uses to guide one's actions.

As we grow in dancing, our awareness grows too. We are able to develop the ability to quickly perceive our surroundings and of movements in relation to those around us, how to avoid collisions on the dance floor, how to read people's body language and anticipate steps ahead. Some are blessed with keen awareness as a gift. That's rare, but it is something within each of us that we can learn to develop. There's no better lesson in life than to observe how that process occurs on the dance floor, because we can take the same process and apply it to our everyday lives – off the dance floor. That awareness is like an invisible guiding hand that helps us through life. And the more we find it and practice it, the easier it comes. Dancing provides a great opportunity to practice quieting the mind, setting aside the distractions, and keeping open the channels that extend our dance lessons to the lessons of life.

Chapter 8

Foundations

A good frame is essential for a solid connection with your partner and a requirement for dancing proficiently. Finding your frame for proper ballroom dance technique is the cornerstone for the foundation of learning to dance well. As experienced dancers, even when we've come to find that perfect frame with our partner, we know all too well how difficult it is to maintain. Any breach in the frame results in a breakdown of the lead-follow connection which, ultimately, detracts from the confidence of the leader and leaves the follower confused. One of the most challenging aspects of ballroom dancing is keeping the connection with your partner through the entire dance.

When something's not right with your dancing, you look to your connection and examine your foundation to try to correct the underlying problem. And just as the integrity of the dance depends on your frame and foundation, your integrity as a person depends on the foundation of your character. At times when things are not quite right in your life, you must look back to your foundation and examine it closely for cracks.

The 'frame' of your life is what supports pure thoughts, proper actions, and appropriate behavior. Contained within it are your character, your integrity, your ethos -- everything that makes up your quintessential being. When things are chronically going awry and the reason is not evident on the surface, look to your 'frame', the cornerstone of your life's foundation.

Very often, we get up in the morning focused on doing the right thing, but lose that focus as the day goes on. Perhaps you found yourself in a situation where you felt compelled to be deceptive, or became critical or quick to judge in a time of stress, or acted self-absorbed when another was crying out for help, or looked back on something you did that was hypocritical. We know the things that go into a good character, but there are always slip ups. This is like letting down your frame in the middle of the waltz only to find yourself with a vanishing sense of confidence or unexplained confusion in others.

Thich Nhat Hanh, in his book <u>Touching Peace</u>, offers the breathing mantra: *"Breathing in, I see myself as a mountain. Breathing out, I feel solid."* As you inhale you think of a mountain with its strength, firmness, durability, glory, and beauty. You think of yourself with all the qualities of that mountain. Then, when you exhale, you feel solid, strong, unshakeable. Worries of weakness, fragility, or inadequacy disappear as you settle into a state of peace and calm. When you can maintain that feeling, your confidence returns – but it is not a haughty confidence, rather a humble one. When you feel like the mountain, you don't feel bigger than the trees, rather a responsibility to protect them. When you're imbued with the mountain's puissance, your feeling of invulnerability is not taken with superiority, rather with gratitude. And so you want to use it for the right actions.

Reconnecting with your foundation requires a certain type of strength and resolve. The image of the mountain is often helpful in that regard. But how is that connection accomplished?

Within each of us is a special place of sanctuary, a sacred retreat of comfort and calm. It is a place to which we turn during times of trouble or chaos. This precious place exists in everyone, although it is sometimes so difficult to find, we give up looking and turn to the outside for help, sometimes attracting destructive forces like recreational drugs, junk food, or binge shopping – things that masquerade as a place of peace. Our attention is often drawn to the loudest noises, the areas of biggest commotion or excitement, the exigencies of turbulence, even though these things turn out to be mostly 'surface chatter'. Wisdom, lucidity, and awareness quietly live out of sight, in the depths, just waiting to offer you refuge. If you keep looking – through meditation, introspection, quiet reflection – that place will show itself. And you will find the path back to it easier each time. The more you visit, the more you will find the subtle beauty embedded in its every corner.

You will find that this special, precious place has everything you need for repairing the cornerstone of your foundation. That is the place with the workbench and all the tools you need to repair the cracks in the foundation. And once you become comfortable there, you will want to return often for periodic cleaning and maintenance to keep your foundation strong, thereby preventing future cracks. When your maintenance and repair work are done through peaceful breathing, you again feel like the mountain in your awareness of the strength of your foundation. When you exhale, you become refocused with a reinforced resolve and back on the path where everything once again clicks.

    When you dance and find that your frame or connection with your partner has fallen off, be mindful of the process to reconnect. The more you practice, the easier it becomes, and you soon gain the appearance of smoothly gliding across the floor so that even the few inevitable momentary lapses become nearly unnoticeable. The same approach can be used when you encounter challenges in everyday life by learning to quickly access your internal workbench filled with the right tools for restoring the foundation of your character. You emerge again with all the qualities of the mountain, and ready to take on the daily burdens that once seemed so heavy.

CHAPTER

9

Syncing with the Universe

Imagine this: you get in your car to meet a friend, run an errand, or attend a meeting. You're upbeat, excited, keen, wide-eyed. Your engine's humming, your car's clean, and you have a full tank of gas. As you move through traffic, the cars part almost as if to let you through. All the red lights turn green just as you approach. Your favorite songs come on the radio without a commercial break. When you arrive at your destination, you find a parking space right at the door, then you meet someone who gives you some good news. You feel like you're in a groove and just enjoying the moment. Synchronicity...have you ever experienced it? Every wave and cycle that affect your life peak at the same time. It's a powerful feeling.

It happens. But only often enough to let us know it exists, and that it's a moment to cherish and enjoy.

Scientists studying fractals have discovered a complex underlying order to most seemingly chaotic phenomena. Many of us view our lives as a bit chaotic at times, yet the beauty of the underlying order is most magnificent. And when we're in tune with that sense of order and flow with it, amazing things begin to happen. Even events normally considered beyond our control begin to flow smoothly with our lives. Albert Einstein noted that these phenomena have little to do with intellect: "There comes a leap in consciousness, call it intuition or what you will, the solution comes to you and you don't know how or why."

If you've been dancing long enough, you've probably experienced this synchronicity on the dance floor. Just as you approach your favorite dance partner, your favorite song comes on. You dance with the beat, flow with the music, syncopating and pausing at just the right moments. You and your partner seem to read each other's minds, almost like you've been dancing together for decades. Just as another couple cuts in front and blocks your progression, you react by doing a picture step, and what do you know, the music stretches out perfectly for an extra measure or two to accommodate it. Those watching are awed, while you know there's some controlling power beyond your apparent musicality genius. But you feel in a groove and flow with it, knowing it won't last, but enjoying it as if it were timeless.

There's no formula for creating such moments. They come for the taking, then disappear. But their random appearances may have some underlying order. The question is how do you tune into and flow with an order you can't see or discern? It seemingly becomes harder to find the more you search. Maybe you must rely on your training and practice. Or watch your conditioning and nutrition. Perhaps it's related to your attitude. Or in the aura you create by the way you dress, walk and interact. Most likely, it's in the confluence of all of these things, and more.

Your awareness of your surroundings on the dance floor is not separate from your awareness of the natural rhythms of life. Learning to let your life flow freely and harmoniously with the forces of the universe is the same process as learning to dance to the beat of the music. When you can synchronize the beating of your own heart to the natural pulses surrounding you, things begin to flow together, as if you're a part of a bigger whole. Don't you feel dancing is much easier when the music moves you, rather than you trying to move to the music? Perhaps the key to synchronicity is listening to the pulse around us, then letting it move us.

Synchronicity. Whatever the key to finding it, once experienced, you'll always be looking for ways to get it back...

CHAPTER

10

The Nature of Beauty

The dry, barren cliffs, which so regally act as an embankment separating the Southern California highways from the ocean, become a captivating force as I'm driving one timeless summer day. They appear as huge mounds thirsting for the slightest drops of humidity in the air, the type which came in such abundance in the coastal 'June gloom' just a few months earlier. That is the season when a great natural phenomenon occurs: each day without fail, the wind, the humidity, the temperature, the ocean conditions all convene in a conspiracy to create a cloud covering imperviously encasing the entire coastal fringe just west of Interstate 5, and lasting well into the afternoon, if not all day. As these June clouds feed those thirsty hills, up spring the most beautiful wildflowers of crimson and magenta and yellow, exquisitely adorning these now barren hills.

Beauty is one of those intangible nouns whose definition is decidedly fuzzy. Recondite as it is, we know it when we see it. And, yes, it is 'in the eyes of the beholder'. Why does something's beauty so readily shine for some eyes, but remain hidden to others? In part, because the perception is colored by the observer's life experiences and her ability to integrate that perception with a more general perception of the world. Yet there are still things thought of as 'beautiful' by most everyone.

There is something very beautiful about a hillside covered with wildflowers in full bloom. The sight grabs you, tugs you, pulls on you to draw near. It is all about the intrigue of the relationship of the beauty of a collective entity with that of the individual members comprising the collection. What is it that transforms a fragile raindrop into a powerful ocean wave? But there is beauty in both fragility and puissance. Can the beauty of a serene lake be compared to the beauty of the raindrops that formed it? The beauty of a forest in the distance to the trees which compose it? Or to its leaves, limbs, roots, or cells which carry out the photosynthesis?

 Somehow, in this transformation of beauty from the individual to the collective is where the purest essence of life resides – in the synergy formed by the harmonious union of individual entities. An electron exhibits an innate beauty, viewed by a physicist or thought of from a purely abstract perch. There is a different type of beauty in electricity – the synergistic movement of a harmonious combination of electrons. Form and function combined, seemingly losing the characterization of the beauty of its parts. In both you see life, but only in between can it truly be lived.

 In the springtime, whenever I drive past those lovely cliffs dotted with patches of bright colors, the flowers beckon me to stop and take a closer look at just one of those flowers in detail. They instill a want in me to isolate just one entity of that patch and demand of it: what special quality is it that transforms your beauty from an individual to a much grander beauty in combination with others when observed from afar? And why? And from where does the synergy arise – from the individual entities, or from some outside force – or from within the perceiver?

    I'm imbued with the desire to touch that flower, to hold it, to feel its petals, to examine its structure and smell its fragrance – to discover its beauty in fullest detail, to live with it and become it, just for a flash of a second, then to know by living it the transformation which occurs from the flower's beauty to the hillside's beauty, from the individual entity to the harmony of the collective group, from the mortal to the immutable – all in one delirious instant of pure being.

    How many times have we watched a performance of an elegant dancer with a shiver of excitement just as the smile, the eyes, the grace of the posture come together in a simple oversway measure when the note in the song stretches out, and just before exploding into the next notes which take the dancers halfway across the long side of the floor in two powerful measures? It's like we take a video in our mind, but pause it at one point as if it's a still photograph. Beautiful! But so too was the moment just before. And just after. That video, a collection of successive still moments each as beautiful as the flower, now becomes the hillside – the performance of a different kind of beauty comprised simply of a series of still photos.

Isn't this the essence of our quest to discover what our lives mean? Painting a life of beauty from a collection of days, each with its own unique beauty. And at the instant we breathe out our last breath upon entering the nano-moment spanning life and death, that is when we face the transition from the individual back to the collective, led by the spirit which vivifies life – giving you your smiles, tears, joys, and defeats – and that is when we become one again with the universal divine nature. In that instant, all becomes clear.

This moment is simply what we live our whole lives for. Yet it so richly displayed every time we view a hillside of flowers, and so well-rehearsed – every time we dance.

♋

Chapter 11

Hey, By the Way, Thanks!

When you think of all that dance has given you, how do you say 'thanks'? How do you describe the feeling of abundance in your heart for many of the most cherished moments of your life? You express that through your dancing which says:

Thank you, Dance. Thank you for you, for your ubiquitous and abiding presence. And for each of your pieces so coherently composing you – the open floor, the friendship of dancers, the uplifting music, the challenge of learning, the gracious host, the patient instructor -- the total ambience. Thank you for the gift of being there for our seeking, without imposition or coercion, but to be found from desire and inspiration.

Thank you for this most amazing dance, for the striding humming spirits of movement, and a mystical dream lost in music, and for every vibrant moment which is being, which is infinite, which moves in stillness and sways in awe. Thank you for the unlocked doors leading to the floor, and the lights breathing sunshine on the melody, and the hovering spacious air gracing the moment, and the continuity of interruption balancing the notes intertwined with silence. And in our moments when the learning comes not easy and frustrations abound, when we curse you and hate you and turn away, only to return upon recognizing our own mortal shortcomings, it is there the power of your being shines in the light of your welcoming arms.

Our hearts are grateful for your ever presence, for just being there, for being available with your soothing, healing salve cried out for by the unremitting heaviness of daily travails, even while we ever yearn for more. When your lights dim to but a shade without shadow, and your music sings not to the ears but to the soul, and your air provides not heaviness but carries the spirit across the floor, you show the mightiness of your presence and the eloquence of your harmony. Think not for even a second that any moment of your enduring buoyant presence is less than magnificently blissful.

Words can be misleading. It's all said in the way you dance: "Thank you stoic companion, perpetual friend, selfless benefactor."

Thank you.

Chapter

12

Rubbing Your Feet

I had a friend who was a very accomplished dancer. Every day as a child, her father took her to ballet class, and after class he would rub her feet. Before she left her home country her father again rubbed her feet and told her to take care of her feet, for they are the tools that will take her far. Over the years, whenever she danced, she would be very aware of the feeling of her feet on the dance floor and thought of her father. She thought of all the training and discipline he instilled in her as a child, and she thought of his kindness and the warm feelings she had for him. Even as she put her dance shoes on preparing to dance, her thoughts went to the memories of him. My friend's genetic makeup is not the only thing from her father – she held his presence too. Her father's vision and hopes and spirit thrived within her, and this presence helped uplift her dance.

We all, in some way, hold a connection that has a special influence on our dancing. You may not always be conscious of it, but the feelings permeate your body from the feet up. When you rise up on the ball of your foot and feel your toes grasping the floor, or step on your heel feeling the floor support your frame through your entire body, there is a presence beyond your own DNA residing within you that helps drive your body to dance.

Dancing starts when you learn to maintain balance, then walk, then run, hop, skip, jump. From there, every new movement you try contributes to learning concepts of dance. Many of these movements are inspired after seeing performances by dance greats like Baryshnikov, Fred Astaire, or Michael Jackson, or after reading some of the rich history of ballroom dance, or through some unforgettable dance performance you saw as a youngster. Those images are part of what 'rubs your feet' and gives you the encouragement to dance.

There are images too, that are not so evident, that also 'rub your feet'. Each time you dance, you bathe in the energy surrounding you left by others before you. As each dancer's foot leaves its imprint on the floor, imbued with a little bit of the energy that went into rubbing *their* feet, and after thousands of steps, and thousands of dancers leaving just a little of that energy on each step, the floor — and the whole dance hall — encompass all the energy dance has to offer.

When you dance to a choreographed routine, imagine how many lives have touched each moment of that presentation! Someone wrote the lyrics to that song. Someone scored the music. Someone conducted the musicians. And the singers and musicians themselves have each contributed their energy to that production. Someone recorded that song. And someone distributed it, and played it. And a choreographer devoted part of their life to creating a dance routine that expresses the lyrics, the phrasing, the tempo, and the character of that song. And when you dance that routine, all of that energy from all of those contributors help to 'rub your feet'!

String theory, often called 'the theory of everything', purports that all the objects in our universe are made of vibrating filaments of energy. The connections among those filaments tie everything together, past and present. When you dance and become aware of the energy flowing through your feet, it becomes easy to display in your movements all the rich inspiration you have captured through a simple acknowledgement of the different energies that went into 'rubbing your feet'.

At some point you realize that your dancing comes not from <u>your</u> feet alone but from all of these influences in your life, and you no longer see these components as disjoint, but as an uplifting spirit composed of a long line of connections, and you begin to understand how everything is related. The feeling you feel in your feet as you dance becomes the whole, and you realize that every dance, every musical note, and every inspiring story from those you meet come together to create the movement in your body – starting in your feet. You feel in your feet every molecule surrounding them, every note in the music, every movement of the pattern, every feeling coursing through your soul. The history of music you study and the dance traditions you learn no longer are 'history' and 'tradition', but become a presence within you when you dance.

It's not just about the genetics you inherited. The 'dance vibes' you open yourself to have an order and many connections, and they become your canvas to change slightly or paint over completely – at your discretion – using your own creative talents. The final painting expresses your unique dance in life. And it all starts with a mindful awareness of what 'rubs your feet'...

Chapter 13

The Tao of Dance

Just one moment. That's all it takes.

Whenever you become confused about where your life is going, just take a spin or two around the dance floor. It'll remind you of why you're here, what you're doing, and how you are connected to everything around you. Dancing has a way of restoring health, reconditioning a soul, or simply putting you back in tune with the bigger picture.

When you meet dance, you do not see its face. When you follow it, you never see its back. Dance is within you, a part of you, yet it teaches you – not like a teacher, but like an inspiration. It's only when you're quiet and receptive that you hear the music without listening, that you dance without dancing, that you be without acting.

It's a teacher you can hear, feel and see -- without listening, touching or looking at. You can weave and turn and bow and bend and always end up with nothing. Dance teaches us to thirst for more, yet be satisfied empty. And just when you learn to never thirst, you bask in fulfillment.

Ballroom dancing has a grace about it, so enigmatic and expansive, that when you fill the dance, the grace has nowhere to go except within your soul. When you lose yourself in dancing you are gaining the soul of life. When you stretch onto your toes, you have no solid foot to stand on -- grace is what holds you. When you quicken your stride, you travel less far -- grace is what moves you. When your hand holds your partner tighter, your freedom is diminished -- grace gives you assurance. Grace makes you dwell in the outer emptiness even while inhaling the bustling hub where all of the mysteries of the universe are held. Humility abounds. You disappear, yet endure. You are gone, but are everywhere.

There are many things we can learn from dance. But not like a student from a teacher. More like the sky from a breath of air.

And with that breath of air, and a spin or two around the dance floor, all is right with the world...

∽

CHAPTER

14

Soap Bubbles and Phantoms

I remember as a child blowing soap bubbles in the air, then trying to catch them. Something so fascinating about the mysteries they held inside, I just wanted an extra moment for an up-close look. But every time I just about held one of those fragile falling spheres in my small hand, it would break. And every time it would break, I absolutely and positively knew that I would capture the next one and get to know all the enigmas it encloses. I would blow another bubble and watch it floating so lightly, and as I would try to catch it, again it would break. So I blew another bubble, and it broke. And another...

The joys of living came in those moments between blowing the bubble and breaking the bubble – those were times when I really felt alive. Time became non-existent, fatigue was unknown, the bubbles were like phantoms – here now, gone then, so real, yet vanishing with no trace – then the next one, all enveloped in the trust that the outcome would be different with one more try.

That which is elusive takes on increased interest. The shiny, lighter-than-air mystery vanishes before you get to know it or before you're ready to move on, all the while not even realizing the journey on the way to the goal is an end in itself. But you always wonder what it would be like to hold that bubble, feel it against your skin, while looking deeply within at all its awe.

When we select a partner to dance with, it is like blowing a soap bubble. We're with that partner for only a short period before the song is over and the bubble breaks. Yet in our dancing, there are times we find ourselves in the company of someone whose presence we wish to hold for more than just the time the song allows. But your partner becomes like a phantom, not a real person, a sort of bubble of fascination in a passing moment – and we ourselves become ghosts.

    You try so to make it all real, to capture that fascinating bubble – if even for a brief instant. As you dance, you move forward, she back, giving you the privilege of walking in her footsteps. You dance in her movement and inhabit the space she readies for you, and bask in her glow that has lit your way. When you move your foot forward, you let it kiss the floor where she just stood. When your body moves into her space, you feel her aura and enjoy the warmth of the air molecules which just touched her and now touch you. When your head reaches the position where she just smiled the coyest of smiles and performed the most graceful of head turns, you savor the moment as if you're breathing in the lingering perfume of her being even as she surrenders in your arms. You live the fantasy depicted by the words of the music in those three minutes. That is the experience of enjoyment when the bubble stays just that extra moment before breaking. And it is a moment – when it can defy its innate elusiveness – that will always remain with you.

Being able to connect with your partner on a deeper level, being mindful of your presence together, is like gently holding that elusive soap bubble in the palm of your hand. You can take an extra moment to hold its majesty and enjoy its beauty. When we become real rather than the ghost, we see real people around us, and our dancing becomes enriched with all it has to offer.

The dance party is filled with bursting bubbles, and each one we see brings us a sense of aliveness when we dance. But it is the belief that one day there will be a special bubble you hope might linger just a bit longer before it breaks – that is what keeps us coming back. And in those moments of trying to extend the life of that bubble is when you're living in your partner's arms, looking in her eyes, breathing her every image, and feeling that just around the next corner or just before the final oversway, you will have captured the moment before it vanishes, and finally come to know that moment like no other. A moment that simply lasts a lifetime…

CHAPTER

15

Imagine

There's something about a star so near you can pluck it from the night sky and put it under your pillow. A star resting atop a dream – one of those innocent childhood dreams of a perfect world yet to be.

There's something dreamy about that star. Its light emitting the clarity of vision showing the shortest path to your pot of gold. A twinkling kind of light that cannot be duplicated artificially. A vision so much a part of you, a herd of stallions could not wrench it from your grip.

There's something about a ballroom dancer so graceful you can hitch a ride and float through the heavens. Dancing amidst the clouds in search of your highest dream. A dream so noble and enduring it is inseparable from your walk, your smile. A subtle smile from a dancer whose parting lips arc through space with the complex artistry of a simple head turn.

There's something spiritual about the curl of the fingers on her hand that no one looks at – but everyone sees. There's something about a ballroom dancer who moves with the glide of a skater, the wildness of the stallion, the grace of clear water meandering through the endless obstacles on its way home. A grace so fulfilling to make a paradise of its journey and a statue of its movement.

There's something wildly serene about grace and ballroom dancers and stars and childhood dreams. Something irretrievably ineffable yet universally understood. Should all heaven on earth melt to the seas lest we dance our last dance or dream our last dream? For neither are subject to laws, only imagination.

Imagine... Dance... Dream...

CHAPTER

16

On Dance

(the missing chapter from Kahlil Gibran's
"The Prophet")

And a young girl said, "Speak to us of dance." And he answered saying,

"Who of us would seek dance, lest dance seek us? When you dance, it is to fill your need, but not your emptiness. And when you dance you become a teacher, though you know not that you teach.

"The quiet and empty spaces become filled with music. And the music moves forth the vibrations that rustle the soul. The player of the lyre is moved by his heart. But is not the mere quivering of his heart the movement of dance?

"Even the shepherds say the dance will come in due time, when it is ready. The dance will rise in its wings to the tempo of the sun's daily journey. And at night, follow the moon's glowing path. When you dance you are a harp through whose soul your sorrow turns to music. Which of you would pluck a single string, when together they dance in unison?

"At the noon's sun or darkness of midnight, the dance arises from the stirrings of the soul. When the feet move – it is not just the feet, but truly all things move within your being: the light and darkness, the desire and fear, the peace and discontent. Dance is life when life reveals her many mysteries. The mysteries deeply hidden in the soul stand naked in the music and become adorned by the beauty of truth. It is where darkness is shed, lifelessness becomes energy, the tainted becomes holy. And when you have found truth, speak it not with words which come from the voice, rather with the dance which comes from the soul. Words are but a cage entrapping their meaning. When your heart speaks through your dance, the cage is unlocked, and all the world listens."

Then he looked at the girl with her bright eyes and innocent features and said in barely a whisper:

"The solitary path to dance is but through the vibration of the music. The music begins. The dance follows. And nothing less than the essence of life is what happens in the moment between. If the white eagle could still that moment, it is there you would find an answer to your life's yearnings.

"Dance will find you, you need not seek it. It is already within, but awaits the ether in which to flow. Look not for the ether, it is not what you would see nor the music you would hear. Rather, the ether you see even in blindness, and a rhythm you hear even in deafness. Only when you sip the nectar of silence will you hear the music, and when you have reached the heavens, then you shall begin the journey, and when life claims your limbs and refuses to catch your fall, then shall you truly dance."

Chapter 17

'Selfish' Giving

I once heard someone say that dancing made her feel alive, it gave her confidence and the freedom of movement, and allowed expression of something inexpressible in words. She said "This is one thing I'm doing for myself."

We don't often realize that some things we view as selfish, i.e., that we do for our own self-interests, are really very selfless acts. When you dance you never know who is watching, and what emotions your dance evokes in that person. The enjoyment by others of watching your movements in dance is rarely recognized or adequately communicated, but you should realize you do bring joy to others just by that selfish action of "doing it for yourself".

Countless times I've witnessed onlookers smile at someone performing or become immersed in a dancer's movements, I can only imagine the sparks going on inside. Might one not be motivated to learn to dance from watching you? Or be inspired to open a creative door in their life because they saw you doing something for yourself? To paraphrase writer Zig Zigler, "you never know when one act, one 'dance' of encouragement can change a life forever."

Once I was arriving for a ballroom party already in progress, and as I approached the venue, I saw a very elderly lady slowly ambling down the sidewalk outside with the help of a walker. She had stopped in front of the studio and was watching the dancers intently through the front windows. As I neared her I saw a beautiful gleam in her eyes and a smile come to her face, and wondered if perhaps she was a ballroom dancer in her youth. I imagined what fond memories she was reminded of. Whatever it was, it brought a moment's pleasure to the day of at least one person, even if vicariously, and brought that happiness through a selfish – yet really selfless – act of some dancers.

CHAPTER

18

The Beauty of Entanglement

I sometimes wonder if I was destined to sit at a desk late into the night unravelling a seemingly random set of data, trying to make sense of it. I suppose I have a history of such drudging acts.

When I was a boy, my father taught me how to make a kite from balsa wood sticks, some old newspaper, string, and homemade paste using a mixture of flour and water. Elmer's glue hadn't been invented yet, and we were on a tight budget. I would always get a rag from an old tee shirt to make a tail for the kite – it never seemed to fly right without one. I'll never forget how easy it was to tangle up the ball of string after the inevitable first crash of the kite. I saw other kids fly kites, and they too got their strings caught in the trees and ended up in a tangled mess. But they would usually give up in frustration and walk away, perhaps asking their mothers to buy them another ball of string.

I developed a fascination with the art of untangling that string, which seemed to have its own unique sense of recalcitrance. That tangled string would seemingly sit there laughing at me as I pondered how such a mess could "just happen". I pensively wondered if I could get that string tangled up and knotted if I tried – or if such a tangled mess could only result from 'not trying'. It occurred to me that it would be easier to untangle the string if I knew how it became tangled. And when I inevitably untangled that string, often after long and frustrating moments, a great sense of accomplishment permeated my disposition. But more, and this may sound crazy, I recognized a sense of beauty in that unjumbling process – an act of organizing, making useful, adding value to something seemingly worthless.

Little did I know that there was a formal study of 'entanglements' known as knot theory, a part of the branch of mathematics called topology. Like many new developments in mathematics, knot theory was developed from a strictly theoretical aspect, and later found applications in such things as the structure of an atom. As a youthful kite string knot detangler, I was unwittingly participating in some of the rudimentary practical aspects of knot theory. This adventure seemed to be so much a part of my DNA, I went on to get my college degree in mathematics, ending up in a lifelong career as a data scientist tasked with trying to unjumble large data sets in search of patterns, trends, correlations, and associations. Very much like untangling a jumbled ball of string...

When I saw the other kids walk away from their tangled ball of string, it made me sad...and introspective. Did they not see the beauty in unravelling a jumbled mess? Or feel the reward of rendering something useless useful? Or the beauty in giving new life to that which had lost its function? I also saw, in a rare instance, others who had the patience, the perseverance, and the dedication to achieve such moments by untangling issues they confronted in their lives – not necessarily a ball of string, but a nagging problem, a complicated decision, or a life altering conundrum. And these observations have given me even greater strength and a deep sense of commitment to persevere through the travails of life myself.

I had never been surrounded by many who were resolved in a commitment of persistence sufficient to untangle complicated personal issues. Such people were out there, somewhere. I heard of them, saw them in movies, read about them, and occasionally met one or two. We just never seemed to cross paths often or become involved in each other's lives; such are the consequences of introversion, a hallmark of many a 'disentangler'. But I gained momentum to continue untangling by the simple awareness of their presence.

Whenever I was confronted with a problem of my own, I would go off by myself and think about it from every angle I could until a solution would show up. Then I would ask if there might be other solutions. And which is the best. I didn't always come to a solution, and when I did I was never sure it was the best one. But things worked out ok. By the end of the process, I usually felt like the boy in me proudly holding a ball of string I managed to untangle. My thoughts often turned to how to prevent the string from tangling up again.

During my decades of dancing, I've met those who developed some bad habits in their technique. It's not uncommon to 'miss' something as a beginner taking dance classes, but still wanting to move on to more advanced classes instead of repeating the basics until they are perfected. Many want to advance too rapidly and dance those advanced patterns after watching more advanced dancers moving through them with such ease. Some with little discipline omitted the necessary practice at what they learn at the basic level. Sometimes there is a miscommunication during the instruction. There are many ways bad habits develop, and it happens to most of us. Those who catch the errors early can correct them before they crystallize into a habit. Some who don't, end up practicing those bad habits year after year. After a while, the poor technique gets ingrained in muscle memory, it slows down the learning process, and ends up putting severe limitations on the level of dancing skills one can attain. It becomes so hard to unlearn those poor techniques and relearn them the correct way. Much like untangling a severely tangled up ball of string. And like the kids who gave up on the string and just bought a new one, many of these dancers just keep adding more and more advanced lessons thinking that will solve their problems, it being way too much effort to unlearn the bad habits and go back to the basics.

If your dancing isn't going where you want it to, and you've tried everything to get past the blockade, try one more thing. Go fly a kite! And when the string tangles up, take a deep breath and untangle it. It helps develop focus, patience, and a growth enhancing introspection not available from classroom erudition. And, it can lead to a new way of life, not only helping to correct your dance technique, but also providing a template for solving personal issues of all kinds.

☙

Chapter 19

Monster in the Mirror

There's a time, or at least a moment, in every man's life when he feels invulnerable. The dragons have all been slain, the fires extinguished, the poisons rendered impotent, and the horizons crossed. He has nothing left to conquer. He stands upon a mountaintop in righteous defiance of his own frailties, in challenge to the gods, unaware even in that fleeting moment of the cancers creeping unseen within the core of his being.

Yes, fleeting is that moment, for in the next, he realizes the dragons have simply changed costumes, and that horizon was merely a mirage. That's when a cold, dew-filled morning with a hint of red skies and an eerie stillness grabs him by the throat and stands him up, gazing at him with a stare that could petrify an iceberg, shooting a monstrous look which makes the last of his courage bleed to the bowels of the sewers. And if he happens to have been there before and gets tired of running, one time he looks back in the eyes of the monster, unable to look away from the naked truth, suddenly realizing that monster is in the mirror.

That's when he admits it. He's a junkie, an addict. He's strayed from the straight and narrow. He's lied, deceived and cajoled to get his fix. He often goes through years of denial, almost daily saying to himself he could quit anytime he wants. But who was he fooling? Finally, slowly, he realizes he should have listened to all those warning signs along the way.

You're never quite sure of the exact moment you get hooked. For me, it's been too many years to count. And my addiction to ballroom dancing has never abated. It's been a one-way street in a maze with too many turns to remember how to get back. Early on, I got rid of all my living room furniture to have more room to practice at home. That was a big warning sign right there. Addicts tend to be one-track minded. Then there were the times I'd sneak out of work early to make that all-important dance lesson on time. I can't even count the times I left out of town guests stranded while I rushed off to the weekend party to get a fix. The guilt – oh help me!! Yet you become good at hiding it. You store it in a deep recess of your soul – somewhere with a type of switch you can use to control it – ON for lucidity to justify it. OFF for darkness to forget it.

I've seen my monster. I've drawn my sword. And as I grab that demon by the hair, raising my sword toward the jugular in finality, he reminds me that I'll be late for the dance party. I look at my watch, then at his sorry smirk. Then at my sword. Then at my watch again.

"Er, could you excuse me?" I said, dropping my sword. "I'll be back in a few hours".

♥

CHAPTER 20

Guru of Dance

It was a grueling week in the blistering cold wind and icy snow when I made my way up the peak. There were countless lonely nights wondering if I would first fall off a cliff or freeze to death. But unswervingly driven by my quest for the holy grail of dance, I finally made it to the top in search of the great dance guru of Mount Promenade. That first morning he appeared to me with a friendly greeting as he welcomed me to his abode. But I got straight to the point. "What is the secret, Great Guru, of attaining dance nirvana?", I demanded. He smiled – inwardly more than he showed – but I could tell from the gleam in this eye that others, many others, had come before me asking the same question.

He asked me to sit, look around at the breathtaking view, see the earth below, feel the clouds on my skin, breathe in the pure air bathing us. I did, then started again: "Great Guru, I am told you hold the key to finding ultimate happiness through the joys of dance. Please..." I begged, "I have come all this way, could you please share your wisdom with me?"

He took on a stern air of peace, a sense of oneness with his surroundings. He took a deep breath, then slowly spoke while looking off at a great white capped peak in the distance. "My son," he began. I leaned forward, listening intently. "There is no secret answer. It is in front of you – and everyone – for the taking. You ask for a prescription to dance nirvana," he continued. "Look within yourself and you'll find it. But it will take focus and dedication. You know respect – listen as intently to your instructors as you do now to me. You know hard work – practice as hard as was your sacrifice to climb my mountain. Here you can look around and see for miles. Take that image with you -- think of the big picture and the reasons why you dance. Then connect the joy in your heart with everything you've learned. One day, I promise, you will dance a dance like no other. It will be the right partner and the perfect music, and your training will begin lifting you during the dance, you'll feel almost weightless and floating off to another dimension. You'll feel unaware of anything except your oneness with the dance, the music, your partner, your movement. And as the song ends, you'll find yourself safely back on the floor, awaiting the next dance, and the next chance to reach your heaven. I nodded enthusiastically as he looked at me wearing a question on his face: "Is that what you seek?"

    I sat still for a silent moment as the guru finished. And as I looked up, he had vanished. The mountain peak was transformed into a dance floor and music arose from the wind. Without conscious awareness, my feet began to move, then my legs and I was dancing and floating through the space, and I felt the feeling of which the guru described – passing through dimensions I've never before experienced. Lighter than air, I glided with grace, and as I turned the corner, a tap on the shoulder wakened me from my daydream. "Would you like to dance?", an eager young lady asked as she stood undoubtedly wondering why I was smiling so broadly. "Sure," I said, and as we danced, I fumbled and tripped over my own feet, but still continued smiling. "Some day I'll get this," I promised. "Some day!".

♡

CHAPTER

21

Words Can't Describe

What could be more telling than the ways of a ballroom dancer? The movement, the sway, the attitude, the demeanor.

What Pulitzer Prize winner could describe the most intricate details of a dancer's movement in a way that could aptly portray the picture of her passion for the dance, or the strength of your hands which give her balance and caress the grace? What words can paint the emotions which operate the ten-thousand muscles of her body required to perform a hover corte, rumba cross, throwaway oversway, or tumble roll? And when her hand reaches for the sky, or her head turns away knowing you'll hold tighter, or the little finger on her hand clutching your bicep curls with distinction, or her lips part barely a breath's width, or her unquestionable trust that you are there for her, who among those watching could be left guessing about the character and substance of her heart, or yours by providing a safe canvas on which to paint?

    And when you watch her walk or sit or smile – you see the mask, but when you see her dance, you see the mask removed and all her frailties and strengths combine in a magnificent ebb and flow that's inseparable from her heart, her charm, her grace, her beauty. And when it flows through her blood and resides in her marrow and she breathes every movement, then you can taste the lust with her every lilt – that is when you simply want to hold her the way the music demands. And there are no words to describe the color the artist uses to show her desire to be touched that way.

You admire her from afar, or close up, and the thumping of your heart gains momentum as you take her hand in the perfect dance. Even as she waltzes, her halo emits a glow that covers her in a spotlight for all to see. Her eyes sparkle in that glow and her innocence becomes magnified.

How often have we seen it, felt it, when we see her on the floor – that feeling which comes between the heart and the intellect, somewhere inside us that makes the words 'romance' seem way too broad and 'awe' seem way too inadequate. Can anyone but a ballroom dancer evoke such a recondite reality, then so nonchalantly walk off the floor returning to her mask to cover that mystery she doesn't want you to see -- even when we all understand it perfectly? Only a ballroom dancer can.

It is the gift that can only be understood without words, painted so vividly on a canvass called the dance floor under a spotlight emanating from desire—a gift only she in the dance and you in her presence can imbue with value. This is your life. For these are the ways of the ballroom dancer. Ways we all know, but can't seem to put into words...

Chapter

22

Showcase at the Seashore

It was a late Tuesday morning, midway between my own last and next dance, as I stared, mesmerized by the performance on the now-abandoned beach before me. The water was a glowing azure, the air fresh with life, and ripe for the picking were images of the shore's showcase marked by the sea's scribblings in the sand below. My perch from the low bluffs afforded me a strategic view of the bustling activities all around. And I took in with passionate intensity that which others pass by as inert. It took only moments to realize those scribblings had an order about them, much as a quickstep – appearing random to the untrained eye – has its own.

    A wave lapped gently onto the sand, playfully performing a foxtrot whose movement powered the glistening bubbles at the water's leading edge into a hover, then grapevine, then ebbing in retreat with a reverse wave leaving the bubbles behind to break, but only after a momentary pause to take their bow. A new surge came. With a final push up onto the sandy beach, the wave broke into syncopation with three smaller wavelets – cha, cha, cha... A bit farther out, a steady, driving wave whose white caps evenly tangoed forward with unstoppable determination, breaking into a roar of passion then ebbing in a quiet resurgence. I looked a bit North just as the next wave broke over an imposing rock jutting up from the sea's floor, flawlessly performing acrobatic aerials the likes of no swing dancers I've ever seen. Well, those waves! They've had enough practice ... how many millions of years?

Twelve tiny terns danced in unison in the sand, chasing then retreating from those fragile breaking bubbles, choreographed by a simple desire to play. The sea breeze which escorted those waves continued on to the dunes, there creating in the white sand furiously rotating miniature eddies which waltzed around the dried kelp on shore. The wind whistled its tune and the sea was alive. This was one of Nature's dance studios, the waves – its dancers, the sand – its dance floor, and the roar of the wind and ocean – its music.

There's no promotion or advertising for this showcase. The performance is free and open to all, 24/7. But, 'shhh...'! Consider it our little secret.

CHAPTER

23

The Spirit of Dance

Great dance parties are like a chemical reaction. They require the right ingredients plus a catalyst to make it all happen.

We all know the ingredients: good music, intelligent mix, conducive atmosphere, momentum, attitude, consistency. And these things are brought about by the unspoken contract between party host and attendee. The host provides a safe, friendly environment

– the attendee brings a smile and open attitude. The host provides the decorations and lighting conducive to the mood – the attendee dresses nice and looks good. The host plays excellent music, the attendee dances his best and mixes with the crowd with the proper ballroom etiquette. The host provides refreshments, entertainment, and the opportunity – the attendee pays a cover charge, brings good cheer, volunteers to help out, and makes the most of the experience. This is the contract we all make when we dance.

But the soul of a dance party comes about through the catalyst that makes everything come together. This is the intangible portion of a party that cannot be described in words, and has no algorithm to formulate its duplication. A party's spirit comes through the energy created through the interactions of the dancers, the music, and the atmosphere all acting in a type of symbiosis which eludes even the most meticulous planning. We can't describe it, but we know it when we feel it. And when it happens, it is one of those beautiful, uplifting moments that can only be accepted in wordless emotion. The dancers leave fulfilled with a "can't wait" feeling to get back for the next party.

To understand that catalyst, the host must know a dancer's soul.

A new dancer is fraught with frustration and challenge, but there is a time in a dancer's education when <u>discovery</u> overcomes the perfunctory actions of a new student. Discovery is when you know enough about the mechanics and can start connecting the steps with the music. The dance becomes an allure. The experience becomes an adventure. Its enticements become magnetic. Learning to dance is not like taking a required course in college – it is something you really want to learn. There are no tests or grades or diplomas. You show up at every class enthusiastically, eager to learn, wanting to practice, trying to do what sometimes seems impossible, yet never giving up.

With each new lesson, you look forward to practicing and absorbing the mysteries of dance. Soon, dance becomes not an activity, but a place of refuge to escape the stress and doldrums of life. A place of joy and release. A secret place you can turn to for solace. A place you make in your heart for room to grow into the person you are becoming. When the music comes on and you start moving, it becomes a place of freedom – to release, to express, to fly. Ballroom dancing becomes a way of life.

At some point, the weekend dance party becomes the goal – just to get through the week to that Saturday night dance. And on that day, with excited anticipation, you prepare. You want to feel clean, to smell good, to look good, to bring your best energy and attitude. You take out that special piece of clothing you've been saving all week, put a shine on your shoes, an extra bounce in your step, and wear your best smile. As you enter the party, the stresses and worries of the week dissolve, a sense of lightness comes to your heart, you are home. You become excited with the anticipation of arriving at that place of peace you've made inside you – just for you. Such are the allures of ballroom dancing. It indelibly gives you a new piece of <u>you</u>. Like a new organ you cannot live without.

The party host who understands these things about a ballroom dancer becomes constantly aware that, in their midst, as their guests, are people who are forming that sacred place within their souls for the love of ballroom. And in a quest to cultivate that evolving psyche, those organizers want everything to be right – the music, the lighting, the mood, the refreshments, the whole experience – so that when their guests go home, they know they have contributed to their growth in dancing...and helped them find one more color in the palette that paints their dreams.

It's not always about the mechanics of hosting a party, or the unspoken contract with the dancers – it's also about the spirit. And the presence of the right catalyst will breathe life into a spirit that will turn a good event into a great one.

Chapter 24

The Dancing Trees

Ever notice what you dance on? Yo, down here. Under your shoes!

It's me – the floor you depend on when you dance, but never have to think about. The comfortable, nicely sprung, hardwood, glistening floor you all love and have come to take for granted. But that's okay. I'm just doing my job. I guess I'd be a failure if you <u>did</u> notice. Most likely, I'd just hear a lot of complaints. Go ahead, blame me if you're not dancing your best. "Ow, my aching knees! Ooh, too slippery! Just not getting the spring out of the floor! Gosh, Mr. Floor is sticky today! I tire so quickly – must be the floor!..."

You see, my story begins in a former life when I was a tree. Not just any tree. A magnificent, statuesque, towering giant hardwood found only in the most remote parts of the forest. In a way, I felt like royalty, standing on high, with branches sheltering the ferns and other more fragile friends below.

I recall so vividly the happy times I joined my fellow trees in a midnight dance around the moss-covered forest. When stars sparkled in the skies and the wind swept through our branches, we moved freely, happily, as if gliding on air free of any anchoring roots. We would dance all night on those special occasions which never occurred often enough.

Although I had never met a human during my youth, I heard stories of those fascinating creatures. Rumor ran rampant amidst the forest that they too enjoyed ballroom dancing, but oddly enough, they performed their dances on a wooden surface crafted from my deceased brethren. Such were our heroes and the great trees we revered and for whom we celebrated holidays. Since those youthful days, I always had the aspiration myself to one day serve humans as a ballroom dance floor.

I studied hard and practiced often. I watched my diet and stood erect, reaching for the stars. I grew straight and tall, and the rest is history. Here I am, beneath your feet. Did you notice? Well, I notice you. And when you dance well, I'm refreshed, for that is my reward.

At night when you go home and the lights are out, I think of ways to help you improve. But mostly, I reminisce on my days as a tree dancing in the forest. I smile whenever someone asks that age-old question, "If a tree dances in the forest, but no one sees, does it really move?" As if I'm not even there! But if asked, I would unequivocally answer a resounding 'yes'!! And for those humans who don't quite believe, learn your steps well. Behave yourself on the dance floor. Follow the rules of etiquette. Enjoy your dancing without judgment of others. Do all these things, and you will one day see clearly the only logical conclusion: that dance floor you love but never notice is built from very special trees – those that grew straight and tall, and learned the dance well under the stars in moss-covered forests.

CHAPTER

25

Long Ago and Far Away

I saw you sitting on the swing at the park, all grown up, watching the clouds play. You were lost in yesterday. I saw you there the day after the evening I watched you dance, when I was reminded of a vision from long ago and faraway.

Do you remember when we were just kids, and the summers seemed endless? We would play at the park to exhaustion before collapsing by the mulberry bush on the other side of the seesaw where we sat to sip our lemonade...

In those long ago summer days we drew pictures in the sand -- I a train barreling down the tracks headed far away. You drew a princess with a tiara dotted with stones and a gown you dreamed of dancing in one day...someday. We found an acorn and held it up to the blue sky wondering what mysterious world dwelt inside. Too, I remember wondering what kind of woman-yet-to-be lived behind your bright blue eyes.

Today there is a giant oak tree where that mulberry bush was. And I go there sometimes to see if our initials I once carved in the bark are still there. Today there is a beautiful dancer where once stood a little girl with dreams of gowns and tiaras. Sometimes as I secretly watch you dance, I wonder, "what is this power that brings out an oak from a little acorn? What is this power that brings out the grace and beauty of a dancer from a young girl with a simple dream....?"

In your dance I see the passion in your eyes and the essence of your being. An essence fueled by fulfillment and driven by desire, it is a dance that, over the years, has shown you tears of tribulation and smiles of unmeasured joy. Dance has taken you to nothing and made you into everything. When it had given you hope, it broke your heart. When it lit your world, it covered you in darkness. It crushed your spirit and bled the last ounce of life from your veins, it turned you over and around and inside out, and then gave hope back in a new form, and lit your world with a different kind of light, finally stripping away the tears and pain and in the end, filled you with nothing but the simple majesty of beauty, which is everything. It is the blessing, the miracle, merely all which is the elegance of you, trying to simply <u>become</u> – just as the oak struggles for magnificence from its nest within a tiny acorn.

    From then to now, from this to that, something so simple can almost magically become something so wondrous. The world constantly changes under the perfect guidance of that on which religions are built – that which we know but don't understand. But for now, nothing less remains on this new day: simply a brightly colored realization of a vision vividly painted by the dream of a young girl – long ago and far away.

CHAPTER

26

Finding Your Elegant Moments

The beauty and elegance of ballroom dancing are elements that we admire when watching others and that we strive to achieve in our own dancing. But what is it exactly that creates these qualities out of some simple movements? It's almost as if there is some secret formula that is needed to take the steps, patterns and movements we learn in dance class to a level which amazes onlookers and conveys a sense of awe. We learn the patterns and technique of dancing, but there's something else, something that can't be taught, something that is innate to the performer that adds style, class, grace, and beauty to the movement.

It has to do with the attitude, the posture, the parting of the lips, the furrow of the eyebrow, the curl of the fingers, the spring in the step, the bend in the knee, and about a thousand other nuances – all coming together at once. To some it comes naturally, to others it takes hard work. I like to think of it as the elegance of efficiency. When the dancers show a relaxed confidence and move with an ease of style and a conservation of effort, that efficiency conveys a special beauty communicated through grace and fluidity. You can look at it as a secret formula, but it is something that can be incorporated into your dancing only through practice and attention to detail. As you develop efficiency of dancing by focusing on one aspect at a time until it becomes a habit – you can build these habits into muscle memory, just like the patterns you learn.

The more you incorporate these details into your dance, the easier it is to develop beneficial proclivities that will help you in your everyday life. Learning elegance through efficient movement in dance helps you develop habits of focus and attention you can apply to everything you do. Once the discipline you learn in dance takes hold, it changes your patterns of behavior so that those qualities become a part of who you are. And it does take practice! If you strive for perfection in the little things, it becomes much easier to attain excellence in the big things. If you think, act, and behave in a sloppy or unfocused manner all day, you can't expect to suddenly be graceful when you go out dancing. Conversely, by adhering to the focused discipline that dance teaches, your activities the rest of the day will be influenced by the same set of principles, ultimately bathing you in an aura of excellence!

      Have you ever just watched a master at their craft in the creative process, simply conveying a refined sophistication in every movement – whether it be a glassblower, an athlete, a sculptor, or a window washer? I've even watched a master bricklayer with utter fascination! There is such a special type of beauty in their actions which often look simple to the casual onlooker. But it takes years of practice to achieve that type of simplicity which can make a complex task look easy. We could all excel in our jobs or whatever activity we participate in by aspiring to finely hone our actions through improved efficiency in whatever we do. In learning to improve our focus and attention to detail in dance, it becomes so much easier to bring those habits to other things we attempt.

Beauty can be found in so many places. And there are many activities to which we can fine tune our approach in the same manner as we strive for in dance. Wouldn't it be great if we could bring a little beauty to the world just by doing something we love? We all appreciate the elegance we see in dancing, and what a beautiful world it would be if we could incorporate concepts like efficiency learned in dance into our daily activities...

Chapter 27

The Need to Give

I don't know if it's instinct or the nature of community living, but people have a natural disposition toward wanting to contribute, to feel that their actions have some value, that their lives have meaning. We often find that the better we feel about ourselves, the more we want to share and reach out to others. And, in turn, the more we give, the better we feel, and ultimately the greater rewards are bestowed upon us.

There are times in life when you might feel down in a funk – nothing seems to go right, relationships fall apart, you lose direction, you look deep inside and find nothing to contribute. Many of us have turned to dance when things seem gloomy. Dancing is like a shimmering pearl that attracts attention, especially to those curled up in a ball of emotional hardship. Dance tends to draw you out physically and emotionally, helping you to reestablish balance and a sense of being, and again see your life as an ever-evolving process where giving is a prerequisite for further growth.

Each of us has some seed within, some unique talent or ability that can express or create something of beauty or value as our gift to the world. If you're searching for that seed, dancing can be the supreme elixir, a drug free of nasty side effects and toxic addictions – a magical healing potion of sorts. You can look at dance as the symbolic planting and cultivation of what's to come for your life. Drink to your health, then take a look inside and find that seed, no matter how insignificant it may seem. If you can't find it at first, relax and listen to your heart. Move in the direction of what you hear. You'll know when you find it. Nurture it, cultivate it, grow it, then express it. You'll find that others may appreciate it more than you think. The world is not complete without your dream. It is never too late to begin. The world will benefit and your actions may always be remembered...

And the greatest beneficiary of all may be YOU!

CHAPTER

28

That Certain Kind of Dance

There's a certain kind of light that draws curiosity from afar. A kind of light that burns steady and bright, and wavers so slightly in the breeze. It's a warm kind of light that grabs your attention and allows you to feel the nearness of life's far off dreams.

There's a certain kind of path that feels so right. It's a path that leads you through open gates with a whispering zephyr. The whisper is that the destination is no longer important, even as the gentle breeze takes you toward your end. When you find that path, you know it is where you belong. It becomes part of who you are. And there's no enticement for which you would trade it, for there is no want left.

There's a certain kind of way that permeates the air. A way about a person that makes you connect without hesitation. A way that allows you to let down your guard and open your heart, even the heart that has been stapled over with hurt. It's a way fed by every step and nourished with every breath. It's a way we can see, but not explain. It's a way we can feel, but not put into words.

There's a dance. A certain kind of dance. One that happens every now and then — when you see the light, and feel the path, and know the way. And know with certainty there is no other for you. It is a dance in which all the wave lengths are in sync, every molecule in your body is driven by the music and every emotion by one mystical force. You dance your best dance, and smile your happiest thoughts. It is the dance you find in innocence and finally succumb to when you abandon attachment.

When you dance, it is the fulfillment of the dreams you see in the distant light, the path you have sought all your life, and the connections you feel but can't quite explain. When you find that certain kind of dance, it is like nothing else.

Because, for that moment, there is nothing else.

Chapter 29

One Step at a Time

If you're new to ballroom dancing, learning how to dance can sometimes be an overwhelming goal. You see the professional dancers gliding so easily across the floor, looking so graceful and elegant, and think, "I'd like to do that". But upon enrolling in your first dance class you find you have two left feet, and start thinking this will take forever. Many give up early, overcome by the intimidation of a seemingly impossible task – an impression usually generated simply by looking too far ahead.

You learn to dance just like you learned to walk: one step at a time. In your dance classes a new pattern or technique can look amazingly complex at first, but you handle it by breaking down one step, one weight change, one head movement at a time. And when you repeat it over and over, finally getting it right, constant practice will etch it into your brain and allow muscle memory to take over from there. You add other steps and patterns and technique to what you've already learned and after a while, you're dancing goals are in sight!

As dance students, we can see how to apply this same process to tackle any learning situation that confronts us in life, no matter how overwhelming it first seems. Whether it's learning a new language, getting a college degree, or starting a new business – you can approach it in the same way you learn to dance. Even building a complex machine need not be arduous as Henry Ford succinctly noted: "*Nothing is particularly hard if you divide it into small jobs*".

First, break the process down into phases, each of which should be challenging but not overwhelming.

Complete each phase in progressive steps, one at a time. Like dancing, go at your own pace and find a comfort level which will give you the confidence to accomplish the task without stressing out. Just as persistence is your biggest ally, impatience can be your worst enemy. Don't forget to pat yourself on the back with a little celebration when you complete each phase. Then take a breath and start the next phase. Before you know it, you'll be graduating with honors and beaming with the pride of accomplishing your goal.

    Learning to dance can be fun as well as fulfilling. Keep this in mind in anything you approach in life. As you learn, make sure you have some fun built into each step of the way!

CHAPTER

30

Dancing with the Whole Brain

We often look at ballroom dancing as an athletic endeavor arising from the physical aspects of movement, coordination, and athletic prowess. Indeed, many dancers partake of dancing for the exercise and the chance to burn some calories while having fun. In recent years, researchers have found dancing stimulates the brain as well, creating a sense of well-being and even helping to stave off dementia in our later years.

The true nature of dancing requires full engagement of the brain as well as the body, and at the highest levels of Dancesport, both hemispheres of the brain are working together to create a synergy capable of producing some amazing performances. Through the union of one's full physical as well as intellectual capacity, the creative and technical aspects of the dance come together.

When I first began learning the standard dances, which come with a strict protocol of frame, steps, direction of movement, position, rhythm, and tempo, my instructor made a comment that engineers and mathematicians make better dance students since they tend to pick up these aspects more quickly. And it's true that the left hemisphere of the brain controls these technical dance elements, just as it makes for good science or math. The left brain also guides attention to detail, which is especially important in any dance performance.

But dancing would be so boring if it were only about the technical elements. Partner dancing requires equal use of both sides of the brain. Genuinely excellent dancing can arise only when the right brain, in charge of intuition, expression, imagination and artistry, works in coordination with the technician's left brain. The results of a full left-right brain partnership in dance can be amazing. The choreography is always flexible, even in a rehearsed performance, when a sudden intuitive movement by one partner may evoke a truly unexpected and beautiful result by the other. The synergy comes not just from combining your right and left brains, but also integrating yours with your partner's.

Dancing can be a great intellectual activity, as well as physical. When you go to your dance lessons, your left brain gets a good workout. But when you're dancing to the music, don't forget to engage the right brain as well! Your dancing will show immediate improvement, and who knows, you may 'invent' a new dance step without even trying.

Chapter 31

Dancer as Actor

One's expression, attitude and demeanor are essential elements of dance, each dance having its own expression, with romance the common theme. An accomplished dancer will act out the proper role according to the dance in order to achieve the right look. The slow waltz, for example, requires the expression of joyful reverence, living out a fantasy in your partner's arms, as if in a state of bliss. Moving from the smooth, swaying glide to a quick chassé then to the romantic shaping of an oversway, this dance requires a true partnership, the couple acting as one, without a hint of conflict or contradiction. Each dancer abandons his/her own personality and acts out the personality of the union.

The foxtrot requires a bit lighter expression, with a playful, childlike personality at times, but again toying as a couple rather than individuals, perhaps like a boy and girl playing in a puddle in the rain -- but with the grace of a prince and princess. The Viennese waltz has its grandeur, the quickstep has its frivolity. Each dance is a play about romance seen through a different prism.

The tango requires an expression of sternness -- the opposite of joy -- alternating aggression and coyness, playing the part of cat and mouse, conveying expressions of determination and abandonment. The lips part sensuously but never smile, the eyes have a serious look of innocence but never meet with your partner's, except for well-timed, fleeting moments of flirtation. The Latin dances are acted out with expression of overt sexuality, sometimes raw and unfettered, sometimes more refined, the cha-cha with its attitude, the rumba with its emotion, the bolero, the samba, the mambo, each with their unique scripts. The wedding dance of Latin America, the rumba/bolero, is done with the greatest of passions, each dancer acting the part of seductor/seductress. A high energy dance, the samba has its alluring electric sexuality with gyrating hips and grinding movements in which the dancers play a new role, different from all others.

The dance is a game, and an act in a play. To dance is to act -- not just well, but appropriately. The acting role in a tango will never work in a jive, swing or quickstep. To take your dancing to the next level, think about your acting skills – the dance floor is your stage, the audience the camera, and the script, well you can make that up as you go!

CHAPTER

32

The Valley of Perpetual Dance

The darkness came at first, then a soft glow before the lights became dizzyingly bright, then cloudy with a twirling blur and finally clear. My eyes slowly opened, and the vision came into focus. I had just fallen, slowly, silently, like a feather floating to the ground – I know not from where – to an unfamiliar place my eyes now behold. It is a secluded nook deep in the midst of a lush valley surrounded by sheer walls of granite rising from the earth's core. The green mosses and ferns cover the natural walls, and powerful fusillades of water resolutely fall to the clear pools below. The stillness of the water, the strength of the rocks, the peace among the foliage – all bring a quietness to my being, and I, seemingly for the first time, take a deep breath of this fresh sylvan air.

     Suddenly, a distant noise stills me, a dull roar, a constant drum beat and now more curiosity. Where am I? I follow my ear around a bend, through a narrow well-trodden path, and the noise becomes clearer and sounds melodious. It is music! I get closer, and in the distance I see movement. The music is a samba. People are dancing! There is a huge wooden dance floor as wide as the valley spans and as far as the eye can see. I approach. Everyone appears happy and without a care in the world. It's an unending dance floor with perpetual music and non-stop fun. "Did I die and go to heaven?", I wondered.

     The music echoes off the mountain wall and changes to a foxtrot as I approach the floor. Taking a partner I swing and sway with the ease of floating, almost skating, gliding to a beat which now reverberates through my soul – moving through the lush gardens and meandering amidst the waterfalls. Oversway, developé, grapevine, open reverse. And as the music ends, just as suddenly – a tango comes on. I'm approached with casual aplomb by a sultry-eyed valley nymph who looks right at home in her surroundings. "May I have this dance," she asks. As I stutter on a reply and trip my way to her I hear a loud ringing in my ears. I grasp for her but she fades, the music stops, that ringing gets louder.

Darn alarm clock! I sit up in bed, eyes popping open and now I become wide awake. I realize it was all a dream, and here I sit, awake from a dream I didn't want to end.

Now years have passed and that dream is old, but one I recall vividly. I think often of that place in my dream, the dream I would like to have every night, and the place I sometimes wonder – could it be real? "Stop wondering," I tell myself – "it's a mere dream."

But then again, dreams were made to come true...

♡

Chapter 33

Having a 'Plan B'

Many years ago I had a friend who decided to take a pottery class. She spent months learning the intricacies of the process, then got an ambitious urge to create a 'masterpiece' urn for entry in a statewide competition. Being a perfectionist, she spent many weeks designing, then creating her vase. She worked meticulously using the best materials and painstakingly molding, forming, firing and glazing.

Nearing completion, she accidentally knocked the vase off the corner of a table – it fell to the floor breaking into a hundred pieces! Understandably, she became despondent, and saddened for days. Just musing, I suggested she build a new vase from the shards of the broken one in a type of mosaic. Almost immediately, her brain went to work and her negative emotions dissolved. Within a week, she had produced a most amazing piece of art and went on to win her category at the state fair.

We all have times in life when our world caves in. What can we do but pick up the pieces and move forward? Many dancers have experienced this feeling, if not with dance then with a relationship, a career, a health issue, or some aspect of everyday living. In fact, many of us actually began dancing to heal emotionally after some other plan has fallen apart. Some call it 'Plan B'. The ability to change course and see what else is out there. An affinity for flexibility and keeping one's options open.

One of the lessons ballroom dancing teaches us – over and over – is to react to any situation on the dance floor. Navigational skills require the ability to quickly change to a new pattern or a new direction to avoid colliding with other dancers on the floor. We learn to have a variety of options following any dance pattern to maintain good floorcraft and courteous social dancing without having to stop or miss a beat. This comes almost naturally through practice and experience.

So why shouldn't this carry over to the rest of our lives? A river doesn't flow to the sea in a straight line. The most natural path to a goal is often one with bends and twists to avoid obstacles that will surely be encountered if you stay on a straight line. To get around those obstacles, keep your mind open to the idea that alternatives are always available. When you need to change ground quickly, you'll be ready to see new opportunities, change course, and not miss a beat.

The beauty of ballroom dance is that it has so many life lessons. Like learning to dance, life is a constant succession of trial and error. Navigation through the mire of life's challenges has a lot in common with your dancing floorcraft. A 'Plan B' in your pocket can always be a valuable asset! And who knows – it may be the path you were looking for all along!

CHAPTER

34

You Are What You Dance!

We've all heard the saying "you are what you eat". Maintaining good health requires attention to the foods you consume. Many dieters and health-conscious devotees spend lots of time tracking protein intake, adding up grams of sugar, watching fat content, and counting calories. But your diet is about more than what you eat. It's also about how you consume it.

A great diet starts when you shop for food at the market, then moves to how you prepare your meal, and climaxes in the way you eat. When you take that first bite of your meal, you recognize that it's not just your stomach the food is feeding, it's also your senses. You slowly take in the aroma of the moment, thankful for the sustenance that is refueling your engine, and stopping for a brief moment to 'see' the journey that food went through for your satisfaction.

When you eat an apple, you think of its origins as a tiny green bud evolving from the tree's blossom, then the growth of the bud into a beautiful delicious piece of fruit grown under the perfect guidance of Nature's nurturing elements – the sunshine, the rain, the fresh air. You imagine that apple actually knew all along it was meant for <u>you</u>. And it wanted to become its best for your enjoyment! It's almost as if the spirit within that apple wants to become part of the spirit in you. You dine always with gratitude, and the recognition that feeding your body is giving sustenance to the vessel housing your soul. Eating becomes a very spiritual activity.

Likewise, when you dance, you feed the soul with a similar kind of spirit. Dance supports your body with a type of energy required by your soul, that works in conjunction with your diet and the foods that your body needs. It provides the exercise your muscles need to keep you strong, in balance, metabolically sound, and of clear mind. Dance helps build coordination, stamina, the ability to temper your movements between power and grace. The dance you do becomes almost like a new organ created by your body, your mind, your soul. Not so much a physical organ, but a 'spiritual organ'. And the life of that dance grows in a way to reflect who you are. You strive to become the best dancer you can be. And as that dance emerges, the spirit within that dance cultivates a need to become part of the spirit of something bigger.

As the apple strives to become its best for you, there's something or someone for whose benefit you strive to become your best. Ultimately, it's not difficult to realize your place in the universe just by taking in all the stars you can see by looking up to a clear sky on a dark night. We all know at some point that there is something much bigger than we can even imagine that sustains us and watches over us, and provides a reason to strive to become our best.

When you dance, you learn the way to a magnanimous path amongst those stars. And simply become part of the spirit that unifies all that is.

Chapter

35

The Gift of a Challenge

I remember when I enrolled in my first quickstep class many years ago, scratching my head trying to make some sense of it. Surely, I thought, whoever invented this dance must have been drunk! And that belief was reinforced when I heard we'd be doing patterns with names like *tipple chassé* and *fishtail*. Months later I signed up for a new quickstep class. Then another. And another. Still, I was as perplexed as ever. Feeling 'stuck', this was one dance I continued to sit out at the parties as I watched others dance it with ease and grace – I was just looking for a clue.

Years later and with many more months of classes and lots of practice, I began seeing some order in the chaos, and quickstep had become so much fun and one of my favorite dances! And while I'm not claiming to be an accomplished quickstep dancer, yes, it does have some logic to it, and I now look at its inventor as a genius rather than a sot.

Going from being 'stuck' to 'unstuck' can be tricky. We're confronted every day in life with obstacles and roadblocks. Even when things are going smoothly, problems seem to arise out of thin air. Being 'stuck' is simply a state of mind. It's that moment one realizes further progress is not possible without removing the obstruction or finding a way around it. We often throw up our hands and give in to the position of avoidance to prevent further aggravation and confrontation, whether it be in dance or any other part of living. Sometimes a temporary fix is possible, but the impediment remains and will someday again come back to block us.

The perception of everyday problems as a negative force in your life may be the biggest cause of becoming 'stuck'. The first step to becoming 'unstuck' is to look at the problems as a gift! They are put there to challenge you and to offer opportunities – to make you think, discover, invent, to produce, create, care, to make you do the right thing, to mold you into a better human being. The value of an achievement is only proportional to the size of the obstacles preventing its attainment.

If you're feeling 'stuck', be thankful for the gift of a problem to solve, and refocus from feeling 'stuck' to feeling human. Imagine it as a divine conspiracy designed to make you grow and evolve with the challenge. Then look at every challenge as a stepping stone rather than an obstacle. Problem solving is an acquired art. And what better way to learn than with dance! In most aspects of your dance education, accomplishment comes with some patience, persistence, and guidance – and that's pretty much the formula for overcoming most challenges in life. Dance can help us confront our challenges, and by extension, help us learn to handle all those real-life problems with greater ease and confidence.

As far as that quickstep, the perseverance will pay, some day! Right now, I'm just learning to enjoy the challenge...

♫

CHAPTER

36

Not What it May Seem

If you imagine the nucleus of an atom to be the size of a marble, the electrons circling that nucleus would be the size of a dust particle over a mile away. Atoms, which are the building block of everything in existence, are 99.9999% empty space. But when you put a book on a table, it doesn't fall through to the floor.

There are many things about the universe that, in reality, are not how they appear to the human eye. Part of the reason for that is, as humans, our perceptual abilities are extremely limited. On the surface, it appears that the universe is made up of things we can see, feel, hear, touch, and smell, or which we can logically induce from our perceptual knowledge, or deduce from our observation that the universe is logically structured. Limited human awareness of our surroundings does not exclude the existence of more. In fact, because there are so many unexplained phenomena and supernatural 'coincidences', it is certain that there is much more going on in our surroundings than we can possibly know as mere humans.

So it is too in our 'dance universe'. It is not unusual to find ourselves at a social gathering in which we see many familiar faces. You may have been dancing for some time and everyone seems familiar. You may even know everyone by name. But isn't it true that you don't really know anyone in the room, except perhaps for a few close friends, yet we think we have everyone pegged to a tee? The degree that you think you know someone is based on what you've come to learn through personal encounters, your observations of their behavior, perhaps some presumptions, and what you've heard from others. However, we usually only have time for surface level conversations at the dance function, assumptions get us nowhere except in trouble, and hearsay and gossip represent very efficient ways of straying from the truth. There's usually a lot more going on with any one person than what our limited perception gleans from the parties.

If you had the opportunity to shrink down to the size of an atom's nucleus just for an hour – wouldn't it be fascinating to use that time to explore what an atom is all about? But we do have the opportunity to explore and learn about the universe with an open mind, yet many choose to take the easy road of assumption and hearsay. Similarly, when we want to learn about someone we meet dancing, it's far too common to rely on hearsay and gossip and others' perceptions rather than going straight to the source. If you hear something about a person, take the time to get to know the surrounding circumstances before merely accepting someone else's judgment. Two people can – and often do – witness the same event but end up with different impressions. If someone is important enough to talk about, get to know their heart and character rather than their reputation and the labels others assign.

This is an area that offers lots of room for growth, as any of us who have been dancing for some time have certainly been mischaracterized at some point. And far too many of us have perpetrated idle jabber which serves little purpose and ends up distorting.

Whether it be the structure of an atom or the reputation of a fellow dancer, be seekers of truth. It will go far to enhance your own character as well as strengthen the community in which we should all have fun playing.

Chapter

37

Making it Your Own

Have you ever noticed that dancing is not only a fun social activity, but can also be a liberating one? Dancing helps free the spirit, giving you an avenue of creative expression, frequently awakening the sleeping genius buried within your psyche. That awakening can rattle neighboring, lesser known parts of your inner being that have been suppressed and forgotten. Just by dancing you feel lighter from the release of long-time forgotten burdens.

The liberating effect of dancing comes as a result of a stimulation of one's creativity. There is no greater characteristic of individuality than one's artistic or creative ability. That is exactly what brings the flair and style to individual performances.

Ironically, you may have thoughts during your dance training that codified dances are rigid and stifling to creativity. After all, most ballroom dances have only a finite number of patterns recognized by world dance organizations for competitive dancing. The standards and uniformity codification brings to ballroom dancing enable you to learn to dance with your friend in your home town, then dance with a complete stranger almost anywhere in the world.

But we each bring a slightly different style to the dance floor. Despite codification, execution of the dance movements appears very different among us. Because of differences in our body sizes and proportions, the energy with which we move, the placement and emphasis on different steps, the way we perform arm styling, hold our heads and change facial expressions, interact with our partner, or accent our styles with the rhythm, the final production is as unique as our DNA.

Humans have undergone more 'codification' than we sometimes care to acknowledge. We've been described by race, age, gender, height, weight, hair, and eye color. We've had every bone, muscle, organ, and artery in the body identified, named, listed and analyzed. We've been classified by personality type, blood type, and bone structure, and graded on intellectual, artistic, and athletic traits. We've been taken apart piece by piece down to the molecule, atom, chromosome, and gene, then given a number or identification telling us which shelf we belong on. And from all that categorization, standards have emerged which help guide our human development. But when we put all those pieces back together, somehow we miss the uniqueness of the individual, the essence created by the synergy of combinations that cannot be adequately described with averages. Individuals who see things others don't, who dream in color, think in four dimensions, or hear a guiding voice that no diagnostic equipment can detect. Someone who dances a dance in their own unique way.

When you watch a couple dancing and know the judges are looking for adherence to the standards, look closely at the deviations from the standards – what makes them stand apart. Then think of your own life and how you stand apart as an individual. Taking an undiscovered path in life can be scary. But the rewards can be beyond description. Any goal of being normal limits your chance of becoming extraordinary. Sometimes, dancing to the beat of a different drummer makes sense. That's simply the opportunity life offers.

Let the standards guide you, but follow your own creative expression. You may get to release some of those buried burdens, and more – you just might find your spotlight both on and off the dance floor!

Chapter

38

The Timeless Dance

Do you ever notice that sometimes when you go to a dance party, you get so caught up in the fun of dancing, time just disappears? Before you know it, they're announcing the 'last dance', and you look at your watch in amazement with an expression of "What! Already?"

Consciousness can be focused in a way in which Time disappears as a dimension of human life. Such timelessness is a prerequisite to attaining the state of bliss some describe as a 'peak experience' or 'moment of perfection'. These are periods of living of such intensity, times when there is no space between the doer and the deed, that we are unaware of little else around us. This is the essence of happiness, since true joy can be experienced only without wants. Ongoing happiness, therefore, can be characterized by the ability to regularly attune one's quintessential being with the activity in which he or she is engaged.

Dancing can help teach you how to move toward achieving such timelessness in your daily life. When you dance well, you reach a level of fulfillment, i.e., 'wantlessness'. Such a state comes by no accident, but by hard work developing one's skills. The fulfillment is the reward and the celebration of all that hard work, and the more adept we become, the more constant that fulfillment resides within us.

Dancing is an obvious example of an activity that becomes more and more enjoyable as we improve, but the same goes for many activities. Think about the things you do in a typical day and ask yourself, "Am I doing this job to the best of my ability?" And if you could do it better, why not learn and grow toward fulfillment with the pride of accomplishment? No one wants to work at a job in which they're constantly waiting for the day to end. So how do you get in a groove of timelessness at work? Determine what you are good at, then just do it. Once an expert, let curiosity and growth displace monotony. You'll soon find yourself loving your job. The day will fly by and before you know it, your boss will be saying it's time to go home, and you'll be looking at your watching saying, "What! Already?"

Chapter

39

From Deprivation Arises Gratitude

There are times in the bustle of daily life during which we find ourselves reflecting on events of the past, cherishing the moments with friends and loved ones, and giving thanks for all the good things in our lives. Gratitude is not always on your mind, and it is difficult to be thankful for something unless you were once without it. Just as the cost of joy is the heartache that preceded it, gratitude is born of fulfillment having experienced deprivation. Appreciation of wealth can only be genuine as an aftermath of emptiness. When we achieve fulfillment, it is generally not by accident. Fulfillment can come through accomplishment, experience or other type of gain – through work, perseverance and focus. Lack of appreciation can be looked upon as a failure to fully recognize the value of that fulfillment. Because human instinct is to guard and protect that which is precious, absence of appreciation – or the lack of recognition of value – can ultimately lead to the loss of some things that are really very precious. In the loss, we begin building anew with greater appreciation, and in the process learn humility.

    A person's spiritual nature and reverence for life requires a depth of appreciation. A thankful heart is a joyful heart. We're endeared to that which we miss, and through its absence, learn appreciation. What is the desert's purpose but to engender endearment for the oasis?

    You are not born with a sense of gratitude, but learn it as you grow. A sense of appreciation can be developed by taking just a few seconds several times a day to stop and really feel it. Think of the good things with which your life has been blessed – it might be good health, a unique talent, a nice place to live, good friends, the love of a special person, or just some small everyday thing. Then think of a time in your life when you did not have that blessing. Over time, you will learn to take a moment to acknowledge your own fulfillment, and feel the thanks.

As a reader of this book, you have probably found dancing to be a very fulfilling experience. For some, it is at the top of the list. Appreciation of that fulfillment is recognized by returning again and again to the dances, to the lessons, to the parties and dance events, and leading to volunteering your time and energy to give back to the dance community. Often, that in itself is a new sense of fulfillment. Yet how many of us take some time every so often to reflect on what dancing has brought to our lives and really stop to feel that sense of appreciation?

Every so often, learn to pause. Take a moment to visualize how dancing affects your life. Think how different your life would be if you suddenly could no longer dance. Then breathe in the blessings and exhale the gratitude. Dancing is about more than dancing. It's also about learning to appreciate all the little things life has to offer. We all need to find the appropriate avenues to express that 'thanks', and often, it only takes a few moments in a busy schedule.

    Those things that we hold dear help define us as a person. And reaching peace and fulfillment by holding dear the qualities of gratitude, appreciation, and humility is not a bad way to be defined, and something we can find in our dancing and extend to our everyday lives...

Chapter

40

The Night the Dancing Died

The moon was bright that night upon the shore,
A balloon so light, above the ocean's roar
   Where the Dance seemed to vanish as I awakened.
   I wiped my eyes in hopes I was mistaken.
You could have, dear Dance, told me you'd come no
   more,
   You left me confused, bemused, alone, forsaken.

You fled, sweet Dance, disappearing in thin air,
You left no trace, nor reason, nor fare
   And I, having imagined growing old with you
   Sought you once more, oh Dance, and to where you
     flew
Just a wisp of crisp air which left my soul bare
   And memories of all the timeless evenings we knew.

But suddenly, in a brief moment was the proof,
I saw in my last waltz -- I wondered about Truth
   And what it is, really what it means, what life means,
   How to interpret the way life leans.
What is at the core of being, of our youth?
   The dance, the trance, is it actually what's there? Or
     just what it seems...

Wandering slowly along the shore,
Pondering what I could no longer ignore.
   Knowing only loss and dread
   Chilled, aloof and joyous no more, I saw your ghost
     upon the sand tread
The night, the light, the moon, the fright -- what's it all
   for?
   I'm just a mad mind in a crazy head...

Darkness elapsing from a shore far away.
And I, collapsing to a floor of dismay.
   You let me fall from a soaring soul,
   You laughed at me as I lost all control.
With no friend, nor drink to pour, nor place to stay,
   I start each day with nothing more, nothing left to
     make me whole.

The chances now gone, long missed, bemoaned
I became withdrawn, lost in the mist, a shadow disowned.
   And on a secret night I return to this light, where you
      are such –
   With no form nor might nor smile nor touch.
I wonder now, Dance, just for a minute, could you meet
     me alone?
   I once held you so close, but now it hurts so much.

If we met again on a day like this
Without word or play, without remiss,
   No verbs or adjectives to get in the way, nor nouns to
     say.
   Just the sounds of the sea sitting by the bay
Give us this silence – a sweet moment of bliss,
   And the sounds of your music to dance to all day.

And if it felt right,
We could meet again another night?
   Another time, not quite – like the last one when –
   The dance at midnight? Perhaps now or then,
Another time, perhaps in daylight –
   When things might be right, if you return once again.

Glenn Walker has been ballroom dancing since 1998 and writing about it for nearly as long. Since retiring as a data scientist, he's been a leading contributor to the San Diego ballroom dance community through his publications, DJ work, dance party hosting, and numerous volunteer activities under his 'DanceVibes Productions' organization.

Glenn maintains a dance blog site at https://SDDanceVibes.wordpress.com/.

www.ingramcontent.com/pod-product-compliance
Lightning Source LLC
Chambersburg PA
CBHW062110290426
44110CB00023B/2768